AGAPE
AND·HIS
GOOD SHEPHERD

Di Abele

ISBN 978-1-63885-600-9 (Paperback)
ISBN 978-1-63885-601-6 (Digital)

Covenant Books
11661 Hwy 707
Murrells Inlet, SC 29576
www.covenantbooks.com

To James, Molly, Abby,
and all of God's children who want to know the true
nature and spirit of our Shepherd, *Jesus*.
A special thanks to my church family at
Gulf to Lake Church in Crystal River, Florida.

Contents

Introduction

These two stories are about a lamb named Agape and his good shepherd. Every sheep in a flock needs a shepherd to guide and help them through life, just as every one of God's children needs Jesus to protect and lead them down the path of righteousness.

"What do you think? If a man owns a hundred sheep, and one of them wanders away, will he not leave the ninety-nine on the hills and go to look for the one that wandered off?"

—Matthew 18:12

Agape Learns the Way, the Truth, and the Life

"I praise you because I am fearfully and wonderfully made."
—Psalm 139:14

4

Agape the Lamb Is Born in Israel

Agape was born many centuries ago in the land of Israel. He was born in a meadow under a small sheltered area. His mother, a ewe, which is a female sheep, was named Ana-is. She had finally had her very first lamb! Although God gave all animals amazing instinct to know exactly what to do, Ana-is was comforted by her good shepherd being right beside her until her lamb was born. They both checked to see if the newborn lamb was breathing and healthy. He was. The little one was a boy. He was perfect and handsome and marked with one black ear and one white ear!

Ana-is cleaned her baby by licking him. She was so filled with joy! As she looked into his eyes, she smiled and said, "Your name will be Agape, and I will love you always!"

As Agape looked into his mother's eyes, he immediately knew what love was. In the shadows, Agape saw a tall figure watching over them, and he felt at peace and was comforted. With such peace, he began to nurse and fell asleep.

Lambs, like most animals, can stand up and walk right after birth. The very next morning, Agape got up and stood on his wobbly long legs. He was anxious to see his surroundings. Ana-is led him over to meet the shepherd, who carefully picked him up and cuddled him. He smiled, "What's with the black ear, my son?" he asked as he gently scratched Agape's right ear. "You are very unique and wonderfully made," he added.

Agape felt safe with the shepherd. He felt the same love as the love his mother had shown to him radiate.

Agape familiarized himself with all the other sheep as they welcomed him into their flock.

There were many other lambs born about the same time as Agape was. They would soon become his friends.

"He goes on ahead of them, and his sheep follow him because they know his voice."
—John 10:4

Agape Wanders Off the Path

As Agape grew a little, he still stayed close to his mother but was becoming more and more curious about the world. One day, while grazing, he looked toward the bushes where the grass seemed to be a lot greener to him. Agape looked around and saw the shepherd was resting in the shade. He became tempted to go over to check out the grass. All the other sheep and lambs were content where they were eating. Slowly he turned toward the brush area and headed that way. He tasted the green grass and thought to himself, *Yes! It is a lot better over here!* He smiled and started grazing and grazing in the spot he had found all by himself!

The flock was grazing, too, but they were heading in a different direction and moving farther and farther away. Agape was grazing into the bushes now, but he didn't care, because the grass was just as good in there. He thought he was pretty smart having all this grass to himself.

Soon, Agape caught a glimpse of his shepherd, who was getting up and looking over his flock. *I know!* Agape thought. *I will hide in the bushes, and the shepherd will never miss me!*

So Agape ran to hide deeper in the thick brush. He looked back and saw the shepherd counting his sheep! He was amazed! His shepherd seemed to know everything! He was even heading back to where Agape was trying to hide. *He will be so mad at me if he finds out that I ran off!* Agape was worried. *I'd better get out of here!*

Unfortunately, Agape was unable to run. He looked down and found thorns and thickets sticking him everywhere, and a long vine was twisting around his leg. He tried lifting his legs and moving back and forth, but he was too tangled up! The more he tried to get loose, the worse it became. He could go nowhere. *This was a stupid idea,* Agape admitted to himself.

"We all, like sheep, have gone astray, each of us has turned to our own way."
—Isaiah 53:6

8

Rescued by His Shepherd

The shepherd was now calling his name, and that caught the attention of Ana-is! His mother immediately started bleating for him!

"Oh no! Now the whole flock will know what I did!" Agape groaned as he hung his head. He had tried and tried but could not move, so in desperation, he started bleating for help.

In a flash, the shepherd was beside Agape. Slowly and carefully, the shepherd worked at the tangled mess of sharp vines, stickers, and burs that were caught in Agape's wool. Agape was very embarrassed at this big mess! He was holding very still so he would not be stuck by the sharp briars. Finally, Agape was freed!

Agape was astonished! The shepherd was not at all disappointed with him! Instead, he took Agape in his arms and hugged him. He continued to pick out all the briars as he carried the lamb back to the flock. When he reached Ana-is, he placed Agape beside her and only said one thing to him. "Agape," he emphasized, "remember, I am the *way*, follow me!"

On the other hand, Mama Ana-is was not too happy with Agape! She scolded him and let him know how he had worried her! That's what mothers do! Both ways had shown Agape love and concern for him. He said to himself, *I will never stray again!*

"I have no greater joy than to hear my children are walking in the truth."

—3 John 1:4

Agape and Samantha

Agape was getting bigger and stronger every day! He had just been sheared for the first time, and it felt great not having a big wool coat on. He also had his tail bobbed, and it didn't hurt at all! He was so happy, and he felt very frisky on this warm, sunny day!

Agape's best friend was Samantha. She was a lamb who was about a year older than Agape was. They loved being together. The first thing in the morning, they looked for each other. They played and grazed together all day. Sammy always teased Agape about his black ear. "Did you forget to clean your ear today?" She laughed.

Since Sammy was older, she thought she was stronger than Agape. Since Agape was a boy, he thought he was stronger than Sammy. Some days, they would challenge each other. Who could run the faster? Who could jump the higher? Sometimes, Sammy won, and other times, Agape won.

Today they were in a new pasture and spotted a mountain not far away with plenty of cliffs to climb. Sammy said, "I just bet I can climb up to the top of that mountain faster than you, black ear!"

Agape thought of the time he wandered off and did not want to be tempted to do that again! "We'd better not, Sammy," he said, shaking his head.

"Why?" Sammy asked, teasing him. "Do you already know I'm faster than you?"

"Well, no, not really!" Agape retorted.

Sammy shrieked with glee and shouted, "Let's go then! The first one to the top is the winner!"

Now Agape wanted to win that challenge, so without thinking, he ran along with Sammy as fast as he could go!

As soon as they reached the bottom of the mountain, Sammy started to jump from one cliff to another! Agape was right behind her. *She really is a great climber*, Agape thought, *but I'll try my best to beat her*!

Sammy continued climbing with ease, as Agape was getting farther behind. He struggled to follow her but was slipping and sliding. His legs just weren't as long as Sammy's.

"Come to me, all you who are weary and
burdened, and I will give you rest."
—Matthew 11:28

Another Slippery Slope

In no time, Sammy reached the top first. "Hey, down there!" Sammy bragged as she proudly stood on the top peak. "I beat you, black ear! It looks like I'm the faster one!"

"Yes," Agape agreed, with a disappointed frown. "You won."

Sammy immediately jumped down from the top and landed on each cliff she had jumped up. Agape turned around to do the same, but once again, he slipped! This time, he fell down the cliff with a thud.

Sammy knew that Agape was injured by the pained look on his face. As she raced down, she noticed the shepherd already climbing up to help Agape. He somehow knew where they were and that they were in trouble. Sammy ran on, bleating to alert the flock.

Agape was crying because his leg hurt, and it was throbbing with pain. "I know this time I will be in a lot of trouble." He cringed as he saw the shepherd making his way toward him. "I did it again!" he moaned.

The shepherd reached the cliff where Agape had fallen. He tenderly said "Agape, my son, I am here" as he touched his back left leg.

Agape thought, *How did he know exactly where I am hurting? How does he know everything?*

The shepherd took off his outer cloak and tore it into long pieces. He tightly wrapped Agape's leg and gently put him over his shoulders, then the shepherd carefully made his way back down the steep cliff. "You're getting heavy, my boy." The shepherd laughed at the weight Agape had put on from the first time he rescued him.

Agape's pain had lessened, and he was thinking again of how the shepherd was not angry even though he had disobeyed him again. He only wanted to help him. Agape was starting to feel very tired. He rested his head on the shepherd's strong shoulders as they descended the mountain with ease.

"Like a shepherd He will tend His flock, In His arm He will gather the lambs And carry them in His bosom."
—Isaiah 40:11

14

Agape Heals

Ana-is was worried and angry at the same time when she saw the shepherd returning with Agape. The shepherd stopped only long enough to show Ana-is that Agape was safe. He continued walking to the front of the flock, still carrying Agape around his neck.

Agape stayed with the shepherd the entire time it took his leg to heal, and it was a wonderful time for him. Agape smiled and thought, *I have got to be the most blessed lamb in the whole world!*

While Agape was around the shepherd's shoulders, not only was he healing, but he also loved being carried by the shepherd! He heard the shepherd's voice, even his heartbeat. Being that close to the shepherd somehow was soothing to him. The shepherd was so caring to him too. When Agape needed to eat, the shepherd would lay him down and made sure he could graze. He would take him into the water, and he made sure he had plenty to drink. Agape even got to sleep right beside his shepherd. He listened carefully every night to the shepherd's prayers to God. Agape felt so very safe and content.

The shepherd cared for Agape for quite a long time. Agape could feel his leg was better every day, and the time came when his shepherd smiled and said, "Agape, I think your leg is healed!"

He unwrapped his leg for the last time and gently placed Agape down to see if he could stand and walk on his own. After a few careful steps, Agape slowly said to himself, "It feels a little funny, but yes, I can walk again!" He wagged his bobbed tail with joy!

The shepherd took Agape's face and cupped it in his big hands. "Look, beloved, listen to things I tell you, for it is the truth. Do not be tempted to follow others, but obey my word. I am the *truth*.

Just then, Ana-is and Sammy were the first ones to come to see Agape walking again.

Sammy and Agape were delighted to run around and play together. As they ran off, Agape looked back at the smiling shepherd, who had healed him. He was so grateful! He whispered to himself, *Thanks and praise to my shepherd! I will always follow your* way *and your* truth. *I promise!*

15

"So we, Your people and sheep of Your pasture, Will give You thanks forever."
—Psalm 79:13

16

The Additions

After years of being together, Agape and Sammy were still best friends and inseparable. They were not lambs anymore, but sheep! Ana-is had twin lambs, and that made Agape a big brother! Sammy and Agape watched as his twin brothers were being very mischievous, chasing a bunny around the pasture.

"As always, they are trying to find some trouble to get into!" Agape shook his head and laughed. "I guess we used to be like that too!" Sammy agreed, because she now had a baby sister and she was a handful too. Sammy still teased Agape, "They are a lot like you, Agape, but at least they don't have a black ear!"

The shepherd found a great place to settle in for that night. It had stones all around the pasture. He only needed to build a sheepfold at the entrance. He worked on making the sheepfold high, with thorns and briars at the top. This would keep predators away and keep his flock safe.

As always, he would sleep at the entrance with a watchful eye. Sammy said to Agape as she watched the busy shepherd working to protect them, "We are so blessed having our shepherd. He makes sure we are all safe and loved."

Agape couldn't agree more. "Yes! He knows every one of us and thinks each one is special. I think *he* is the special one!" Agape always listened for the shepherd's voice, and he was the very first one to run to him when he called them in at night. It was time for everyone to rest and restore themselves when nightfall came.

Agape's twin brothers, Peter and Luke, had other ideas. "I'm not ready to sleep yet," Peter complained to Luke.

Luke was always up for adventure and asked his twin, "What do you want to do?"

"Let's go out and explore. We can get out through that sheepfold if we wait until the shepherd is asleep. We can find out what he is trying to keep us away from!"

Luke was excited. "It must be something wonderful! I'm with you!"

"Do not be afraid, little flock, for your Father has chosen gladly to give you the kingdom."

—Luke 12:33

Peter and Luke

When the shepherd was sleeping, the twins walked up to the sheepfold. They saw a small opening that only one small lamb could get through. Peter whispered, "Me first. When I get through, you come right behind me."

Peter struggled, and he managed to get more than halfway through the briars. He realized they were much thicker on the other side. "Is there a way to get to the other side?" Peter rethought his escape route. "I am not going to bleat for help and ruin our plans!" Suddenly he saw two slanted yellow eyes staring at him from the other side. That made him immediately change his mind, and he bleated as loudly as he could!

Baah! He heard his twin, Luke, doing the same! *Baah!*

Agape jumped to his feet from a sound sleep when he recognized his twin brothers' cries for help! He ran with all his might to the bleats coming from the sheepfold. His shepherd was already ahead of Agape, and he seemed to have appeared out of nowhere!

It was a hungry wolf that was stalking Peter! He was so hungry that he was not going to let this ruin his meal! He continued to work his way through the briars to grab Peter, who was not that far away. "Help me!" Peter bleated again. The wolf had finally reached Peter! With an open mouth, he latched on to the lamb and was trying to pull him to the other side of the sheepfold. Peter was very scared!

The shepherd pushed his way through. He reached Luke first and quickly pushed him back out of danger toward Agape. Agape ordered Luke, "Get back to the flock, now!" Agape stayed in the shadows behind the shepherd, watching. It was like nothing he had ever seen before!

In desperation, the shepherd forced though the thorns that were ripping his face and body at every move until he reached Peter. He saw what the snarling wolf was trying to do. He took his rod and began prodding at the wolf, hitting him repeatedly.

Finally, the wolf had enough, and he dropped Peter. Peter fell down, and though he was injured, he ran away as fast as he could. That was when the wolf's eyes grew small in anger at losing his meal. The wolf now planned on making the shepherd his dinner.

"And He will arise and shepherd His flock In the strength of the LORD, In the majesty of the name of the LORD His God. And they will remain."
—Micah 5:4

The Brave Shepherd and the Brave Sheep

The wolf was all the way in now and slowly went toward the shepherd. His teeth were showing and ready for an attack. He lunged at the shepherd, mouth wide open and aiming right for the shepherd's neck. Luckily, he missed, and they both fell backward. The wolf was on top of the shepherd and kept biting and growling, continuing his attack.

Agape watched in horror. He wanted to do something to help but was not sure what to do. He did know one thing. He knew that he would never leave his shepherd no matter what happened to him. Then he remembered. He could pray, he thought, just as the shepherd prayed for God to watch over them every night. Agape lay down, closed his eyes, and cried, "Please, God, be with my shepherd, for he is in trouble. Please do not let him be overcome by that wolf! Where would we be without him?"

Wow! Just like that, the shepherd found his strength again. He jumped up from the wolf and grabbed his sharp staff. He hit the wolf several times with hard blows. The wolf howled and backed up from him. The wolf stopped, realizing just how strong the shepherd really was. He knew he would be defeated if he continued to fight. The wolf was injured but managed to back his way out of the sheepfold and limped away.

Agape was so angry at the wolf who had hurt his shepherd. The shepherd seemed to know what Agape was thinking. He softly said, "Don't be angry at the wolf, Agape. He was only hungry and looking for food."

Agape realized his shepherd had no enemies and that he cared for everyone. This made him love and respect his shepherd even more.

Agape then looked at his good shepherd with tears in his eyes as he studied him. The shepherd's clothes had been torn to pieces. He was bleeding with cuts, bites, slashes, and a deep wound.

The shepherd's heart melted as he looked at the brave little sheep who had never left his side, and he said to him, "Agape, do not be worried or afraid. My wounds will heal. Do you not know by now that I treasure my sheep? I would lay down my life for my sheep! Remember this, beloved, I am the *way*, the *truth*, and the *life*!"

Agape knew to believe every word his shepherd said because he was always right. He was overcome with joy, knowing his shepherd was never leaving him.

"The LORD will keep you from all harm, he will watch over your life."
—Psalm 121:7–8

A Blessed Name

Slowly as the sheep and *his master* were leaving the sheepfold, the shepherd said to Agape, "Your mother named you the perfect name, Agape! Do you know the meaning of your name?"

Agape paused and thought. He shyly guessed, "Black ear?"

"No!" The shepherd laughed. "It means much more than that! The name Agape means the highest form of love, the love of God for man and of man for God!"

Agape was delighted to hear his special name and exclaimed, "I'm always going to live up to that wonderful name, to be just like you!"

They saw the awaiting flock in the distance. The sheep were thinking the worst when their shepherd appeared from the sheepfold. He was a sorrowful sight, and they were saddened. They bowed their heads low, seeing how wounded he was. Agape, on the other hand, was so joyful that he was running in circles around his *good shepherd*.

Agape's joy made the flock realize that their shepherd was going to be just fine, after all. The flock began to rejoice in a bleating cheer so loud that it echoed over the mountains. *Baaaah!*

They all knew that their good shepherd was their protector, he was their savior, and most importantly, just as *Jesus* is, he is *alive*!

Closing

Many times, the Bible uses the shepherd and his flock to relate to Jesus and his people. That is because we are like the sheep. We need to be led through our lives by our good shepherd. *Jesus* is our *good shepherd*!

Jesus knew us before we were born. He is always watching over us. When we are tempted, he teaches us right from wrong. When we go astray, he takes us back. He leads us by his word, *the Holy Bible*.

When we are hurting, he heals us. When we are weary, he gives us rest. When we are worried, he gives us peace. He answers our prayers. He is kind and gentle. He loves all of us unconditionally because we are his children.

It's the highest form of love. The love of *God* for man and love of man for *God*.

It's an *agape* kind of love.

Psalm 23

"The Lord is my shepherd; I shall not want. He maketh me to lie down in green pastures: he leadeth me beside the still waters. He restoreth my soul: he leadeth me in the paths of righteousness for his name's sake. Yea, though I walk through the valley of the shadow of death, I will fear no evil: for thou art with me; thy rod and thy staff they comfort me. Thou preparest a table before me in the presence of mine enemies: thou anointest my head with oil; my cup runneth over. Surely goodness and mercy shall follow me all the days of my life: and I will dwell in the house of the LORD forever."

Agape Learns the Ten Commandments

The Shepherd Heals

The shepherd awoke before dawn and rubbed his eyes. He smiled, finding Agape by his side, where he always was.

"Hello, son," he said softly as he scratched Agape's black ear.

Agape made the sweetest sound—a pleasant bleating.

"I knew you would be right here, my little shadow." He paused as his hand touched Agape's horns. "Wow, your horns have grown a lot. They are getting big just like you!"

Agape was finally at peace. During the last weeks, the shepherd was healing from a terrifying attack, having saved his flock from a hungry wolf. With God's help, the shepherd eventually conquered the wolf, who limped away defeated. At that time, the shepherd looked as if he were defeated too. His wounds were deep, and he was in a lot of pain.

From that day, Agape never left his side. Agape remembered being injured slipping from a mountain cliff while racing to the top with Samantha. The shepherd rescued him, treated his injuries, and carried him for weeks as he healed. Agape spent every night with his shepherd, learned his ways, and realized how great this man really was. Now it was Agape's turn to take care of his shepherd.

The shepherd had his neighbor Abram and Abram's son Asher watch his flock while he healed, and today was finally that day!

The Village of Kerr

The shepherd slowly got up with the help of his sturdy staff and stretched. He said, "Let's find Abram and Asher. I need to go to the village today to sell our cheese and buy supplies." He grabbed his large bag containing his wrapped cheese, coins, and his canteen and called to Abram.

Abram was also a shepherd and a good friend. He promised it would be no problem to stay one more day to watch the flock. "Don't worry about anything," Abram assured him. "Asher and I counted your flock, all 118, and they have never tried to stray."

Asher added, "But they sure know who their *real* master is!"

The shepherd thanked them greatly and told them he would be home by evening.

All his sheep were glad to see their shepherd and crowded around him, bleating happily. Samantha ran to Agape and teased him as always. "Long time no see, black ear!"

Agape smiled at his best friend. He surely did miss playing with Sammy but felt he should stay by his shepherd. "I'll see you as soon as we get back, Sammy," Agape said, wagging his bobbed tail.

Ana-is also spotted him and quickly went close to nuzzle him. Agape was a little embarrassed about his mama's affection in front of the flock. After all, Agape was older than his twin brothers, and just this morning, his shepherd told him how big his horns were and how he had grown! Still, Agape admitted to himself that he really loved getting nuzzled by his mama.

The flock slowly returned to grazing, and Agape ran to catch up with his shepherd.

The shepherd turned and looked down at him. "So you think you are going to go with me today?" He laughed. "You really are my shadow!"

Agape eagerly wagged his tail and stepped alongside him.

The shepherd knew Agape had learned valuable lessons of the way, the truth, and the life, and it was always nice having him along. He called out to Abram and Asher, "Make my sheep count 117 for today!"

The two men laughed and waved at the softhearted shepherd taking Agape along.

1st Commandment
No Other GODS
Besides GOD

31

Right outside of Kerr, there was a beautiful stream to drink and a place to rest. Agape jumped in the stream to splash the shepherd, and the shepherd playfully chased him around a bit.

The shepherd then did what he did every morning. He knelt down, saying his morning prayer to God. Agape was going to graze, but he lay down beside his shepherd instead and listened as he thanked the Lord for the beautiful day and gave praise for his healing. He asked for protection for Abram, Asher, his flock, as well as for the two of them.

Agape was curious about prayers, and the shepherd always knew his flock's thoughts, so he explained, "I fulfill all of God's Ten Commandments, and this is his first one. God is the creator of all things and worthy of praise and worship. We thank, honor, and show our love to him for all he does for us."

Agape remembered his prayer to God when the shepherd was in danger. God gave his shepherd strength when he had no strength of his own. *Wow*, Agape wondered, *if there are ten commandments, I wonder what the other ones are.*

Immediately the shepherd, knowing his question, replied, "I will teach all of them to you."

The Large Man in Kerr

Agape had been to Kerr when he was a lamb, but this time, his eyes were wide open as he took in the busy people and animals of all kinds. Kerr had many homes made out of stone. The people there were selling pots, blankets, garments, knives, tools, and different foods.

His shepherd talked and laughed with some friends at the market for some time before he approached a large man behind a table. Agape watched as the shepherd spoke to him and showed the cheese he had to sell. It seemed they were not agreeing about its value, and the shepherd started to walk away. The man called him back, and for a long time, they continued to barter. Eventually, the shepherd handed the bag of cheese to the large man, and he handed some round coins to his shepherd. His shepherd thanked him as he placed the coins securely in his bag.

Then the large man spotted Agape and smiled. He cocked his head and said, "Oh, is your little sheep for sale also?"

Agape quickly scooted behind the shepherd and peeked out at the man, who was still looking him over.

The shepherd placed his hand on Agape, showing him not to fear. "No, sir, I am sorry, but he is not for sale."

The man got up from his stool and ran over to study Agape. He felt his wool and moved his hands all around the sheep.

The shepherd knelt down by his sheep and repeated, "He is not for sale."

The man retorted, "I will pay very well for this fat sheep. His wool is exceptional! It's very soft and actually shines! You will make more money selling him than you did for your cheese." He continued walking around Agape, pleased with what he saw, and added, "He is a very *unique* sheep."

"I agree." The shepherd nodded. "But I raise *all* my sheep for their cheese and their special wool." The shepherd stood up, looked at the man, and only said, "Good day, sir!"

The large man squinted as his smile turned into a frown when he realized the sheep could not be purchased.

Agape was filled with joy at not being sold as they walked off. Then he suddenly stopped and thought, *Wait! What did he mean by this "fat" sheep?*

The shepherd laughed at what Agape thought and told him, "Remember only that he can see how *unique* you really are."

Agape liked that word because his shepherd often called him unique! The shepherd bought the supplies he needed, and they left Kerr.

"Let's rest a bit, Agape," the shepherd said as they passed by the same stream when heading home. "Why don't you graze awhile?"

Agape was hungry, so he started to graze as he listened carefully to the shepherd tell a story.

"You just learned the second commandment. It says you must never make anything in your life more important than God, he always comes first. If you think something or someone is more important than God, the thing you love more is called an *idol*. Many people love having gold, silver, or jewels. They love being rich even more than they love God.

"The man at the village wanted me to take much less money for my cheese than it was worth. I did not want more—only a fair price. I feel that man wants to be rich more than anything else, which makes his riches his idol. I am rich with the things that God provides for me. God's blessings are from a well that never runs dry. He gave you to me, Agape, and I would much rather have you than gold."

Agape was happy to know the shepherd loved God first and he loved his sheep more than he loved any riches. They started home together, enjoying the beautiful sights along the way.

When they returned home, the shepherd told Abram and Asher about his trip. While in Kerr, he heard about a lush pasture three villages away. Tomorrow he planned to take his flock there while the grass in his pasture had time to regrow.

The shepherd cooked a big meal for the three of them. Before eating, they offered thanks for all God had provided. Afterward, he thanked his neighbors for all their help and gave them each a gold coin, cheese, and a garment before they returned to their home over the mountain. The shepherd went to the entrance of the sheepfold to rest for the night.

Agape had been telling stories to the other sheep and lambs about the adventures in the village, and he explained the two commandments his shepherd taught him.

Samantha's eyes got big, and she leaned over to Agape. "Black ear," she whispered, "I am certainly glad you weren't sold to that man!"

Agape liked that Sammy was concerned about him, and maybe that was why he knew she was always going to be his best friend. The whole flock liked Agape, but Ana-is smiled, knowing that Sammy admired Agape as much as she did even though she always teased him.

Agape said, "It's nightfall, so we'd better rest."

He saw his mischievous brothers, Peter and Luke, sneaking away, and he loudly scolded them, "That means the two of you too!"

The flock all laughed as they saw them both returning, knowing better than to disobey their big brother again.

The Large Man Tries Again

The next day, the shepherd rose early. They had several days of traveling ahead. They would be going through the villages of Kerr, Neva, and Zon before they would arrive at the new pasture and sheepfold. He knew he only had to call his sheep one time, and they would all rise and follow him anywhere. Of course, his shadow, Agape, and Samantha were beside him.

When they arrived in Kerr, it was busier than ever. The flock knew to stay together as they walked through the entrance, looking around at the sights they didn't normally see in the pasture.

Samantha spotted a large man behind a table, and he was arguing with a man carrying cages of chickens. Her eyes widened. "Agape!" she whispered, looking toward the large man. "Is that the man you were talking about?" She frowned and moved closer to Agape and her shepherd.

"Yes, Sammy, that's him," Agape said calmly, "but don't worry. Our shepherd is here."

The shepherd reached down to pet Sammy and reassure her. He paused when he heard the two men shouting loudly back and forth. The large man was shaking his fist and cursing the other man for not taking his low offer. The other man had enough, so he picked up his cages and left. The large man got up from his stool and ran after him, continuing to curse him. When he realized that he was not going to make a sale again today, he stormed back to his table, anger showing on his face.

The shepherd was not pleased with the large man's actions and needed to tell him so. The flock stopped and listened as he walked over to him.

The large man saw the shepherd and noticed he had a whole flock of very nice sheep. His frown changed to a wide smile as the shepherd approached, hoping he could make a sale. "Sir!" the large man said in a kind voice. "I see you have your flock with you today. No wonder you did not sell that hefty little sheep to me yesterday."

Agape turned to Sammy and proudly whispered, "*Hefty* must mean 'unique'!"

The large man continued, "You wish to sell your entire flock to me, right?"

3rd Commandment

Always Treat GOD'S
Name With Respect

The shepherd told the man exactly what he thought. "Sir, you are sadly mistaken. I told you yesterday that *none* of my sheep are for sale. I am only here to warn you that there are many small children and godly people in the village. Your actions to that man were ungodly, and cursing was uncalled for."

The man was very surprised and tried to defend his actions by saying, "I read the Holy Bible, and I am a man of God!"

The shepherd asked, "Why do you disobey God's third commandment if this is true? God does not want anyone to curse him, anyone, or anything."

The man realized the shepherd was right and looked down in shame at what his temper made him do.

The shepherd looked the large man in his eyes and said, "You can always change your ways."

4th Commandment

Have A Day To Rest And
Thank GOD Every Week

The shepherd turned to walk away. He smiled as he noticed none of his flock had wandered off. He called to them, and they followed him out of the village as the large man sat at his table, thinking about what he had done.

Agape said to Sammy, "Maybe that man will change since he knows the third commandment."

"I sure hope he does! He's scary!" she replied.

The shepherd added, "Let's have *faith* that he will change!"

The shepherd led the flock through the village to a small sheepfold on the other side where they would stay that night. The sheep and lambs were ready to graze and drink after their long day.

Agape was extra tired from all his travels.

The shepherd knew this and told him, "Go ahead and graze, Agape. I know you are hungry and weary, but tomorrow you can rest. It is the *Lord's Day*. That means that we will spend the day resting, restoring, and reflecting on God. This is what the fourth commandment says. God rested on the seventh day after creating the whole world in six days."

Agape was amazed and thought, *Wow! Six days? God certainly did need a day of rest!*

The shepherd laughed at his shadow's thoughts and said, "Now scoot!" Agape ran to graze with his friends and told them all about the commandment he had just learned.

Helping Vetri

After a glorious day of rest, they traveled to the village of Neva, which was even bigger than Kerr and just as busy. The shepherd was hungry and purchased some food as the flock watched him, awaiting his return.

Suddenly a mother was screaming so loudly that everyone in the marketplace heard it. "Vetri!" she called. "Get back here! Do not run away again!"

The father was also calling for his daughter in a desperate voice.

Vetri yelled back to them, "I told you I want to ride the horse!" She continued to run farther away and into the crowd.

The shepherd noticed the unhappy animal tied to a pole, his ears pinned back and pulling to get loose, and Vetri was running right toward him. Vetri's parents were running as fast as they could to catch her, but the shepherd was much closer.

There's the horse, Vetri thought happily as she ran to touch him. *I want to ride him around the village!*

She had almost reached him when the shepherd surprised her. He scooped her up so fast she didn't notice the enraged animal tried giving her a powerful kick!

"Put me down!" Vetri demanded.

Instead, the shepherd handed her over to her father's outstretched arms.

The mother ran to her daughter, relieved to see she was not injured or lost. "Praise God you are okay! Why don't you ever listen to me, Vetri?" her mother scolded.

Her father thanked the shepherd for stopping his daughter from making a big mistake, but Vetri was fighting in her father's arms to let her down.

The shepherd got closer to her and smiled as he looked into her eyes and gently asked, "Is your name Vetri?"

Vetri nodded.

"And this is the horse you want to ride?" he asked.

"Yes, but my mother and father never let me do what I want to do!" she complained.

"Well, first of all"—the shepherd laughed—"this is not a horse. This is a *mule*. He is quite a dangerous mule at that. If you had been any closer, he would have kicked you and hurt you badly."

Vetri studied the animal that was stomping his hoof and showing his teeth before saying shyly, "Well, it looked like a horse, but he doesn't look too friendly now that I see him up close."

"We tried to tell you that, Vetri!" her mother added.

The shepherd said to Vetri, "Honor your father and your mother, my child, for they love you and they know what is best for you. More importantly, it is one of God's commandments that he expects you to follow."

Her parents realized all he had done and thanked him again for helping with Vetri.

Vetri watched as the shepherd returned to his flock. She watched him call and how they all followed him. The shepherd turned and smiled as he waved at the young girl, who was still watching him as they left the village.

Agape and the flock saw the whole incident, and the shepherd said to them, "That was an example of the fifth commandment. God wants everyone to obey their parents, and let's all *hope* that Vetri will do this from now on."

Agape thought that was a great commandment and said to Sammy, "I'll be right back!"

He slowed up and waited until he spotted Ana-is, who was with Peter and Luke and all her friends. He slipped in beside her, nuzzled her, and whispered, "I wanted to tell you, Mama, I'm sorry for all the times I didn't obey you."

Ana-is smiled. "You really are getting to be quite a big boy!"

The Man Dressed in Black

They were almost to Zon, and the lush pasture was waiting for them just beyond that village. The shepherd was happy they made it before sundown.

He caught sight of a man who was outside the village and dressed in black and who seemed to be busy collecting a pile of stones. He was so busy he did not even notice the shepherd and his flock when they approached.

"Good evening, sir," the shepherd said, nodding to the man.

This startled the man, who immediately panicked. "Oh," the man said nervously, "good evening."

The shepherd questioned him, "Sir, do you need help with anything?"

The man became annoyed and said in a low, rough voice, "I need you and your flock to quickly get through this village! I am expecting my neighbor to come out soon, and you are certainly in the path!"

Agape and Samantha liked the word *neighbor* because they thought of their shepherd's friends, Abram and Asher.

The shepherd suspected something, so he continued to talk. "Are the two of you building something together?"

The man grew impatient, but the shepherd was standing firm, waiting for a reply, so the angry man offered his explanation. "You see, my neighbor is my enemy. He has been using some of my land for his livestock for years. He thinks it belongs to him no matter what I do to him. Tonight I am going to hurt him when he comes through the village to go home. He needs to learn the hard way. So if you don't mind, please hurry through!"

The shepherd did not move and continued his questions. "So you plan to throw stones at your neighbor? What if they hit him?" The shepherd knew the answer but wanted the man to say it out loud.

The man could not believe it. "Of course I plan for the stones to hit him! I told you, he is using my land!"

The shepherd continued as the whole flock watched and listened. "What if he is injured by your stones?"

"I *do* plan for him to be injured!" stressed the man. "That is why I planned this. I will run away when he falls down, and no one will see who threw the stones!"

The shepherd calmly and truthfully replied with his answer, "What you are doing is sinful. To injure or possibly kill a person is against the sixth commandment. More importantly, you are wrong about no one knowing who threw the stones. God knows all things."

The man stopped talking for quite a while, reflecting on what he was told before throwing down the stone in his hand. He turned to the shepherd and offered an excuse. "Well, I guess I'd better not do this. My eyesight is failing me, and I don't have a very good aim anymore. Maybe I can do something another time." He turned, slowly walking away with his head down. He climbed a hill and disappeared.

The shepherd called out to his flock, and they entered Zon.

Agape thought, *Wow, my shepherd just saved someone's life!*

The shepherd knew what his sheep was thinking. "That's true, Agape," he said. "We may have saved the neighbor's life since the man did not throw stones at him. If that man asks God for forgiveness for what he was going to do, we may have saved his life too. God forgives our sins when we ask him."

Agape's eyes grew big as he thought about that. *My shepherd saved* two *lives! My shepherd is so good!*

The shepherd added, "Thank you, Agape, and God is so good too!"

Time Flies When You're Having Fun

Tonight, they finally reached the temporary sheepfold they would be using, and it looked very safe. On the way there, they had noticed the large pastures they would be grazing in tomorrow, and both looked delicious! The flock also had long drinks from a cool stream just a short distance back. It was so refreshing. The shepherd was extremely pleased, too, and they ended up staying for several months.

By then, it was shearing time, and the shepherd sheared his flock one by one.

Sammy was first, and just like a girl, she asked Agape, "Do you like my hair now, Agape?"

Agape was pretty smart and answered, "Sammy, you look good with your hair short or long!"

Agape, however, was very ticklish and wiggled and squirmed whenever he was sheared. It didn't always come out looking even. This time his hair was sticking out—long in some places, short in others—and one place was shaved so closely that you could see his pink skin.

"Nice haircut, black ear," Sammy teased when he was finished.

They both laughed but loved leaving their heavy wool behind no matter how they looked.

The shepherd had always been told he has best wool around. He bagged it up and put it on a cart he had made. Tomorrow, they were heading home, and he hoped to sell the wool in Zon.

Love Thy Neighbor

As they approached Zon on their return, the village was filled with noisy laughter, and it was crowded with people. Upon entering, the shepherd noticed a girl dressed in white, dancing with a handsome man at the center of the village.

"It looks like a wedding," he said smiling.

He thought it might be better to take his flock around the outer village so he would not be disturbing them, when a man ran to him, saying, "Sir, I recognize you! You were here a while back with your flock, and you stopped me from making a terrible mistake that night."

The shepherd knew him; it was that man who was dressed in black and who had collected the stones.

The man was excited, saying "Come, come with me!" as he led the shepherd to a table where he had been sitting.

"Shamar!" he said to a man seated at the table. "This is the shepherd I told you about. Shamar is my neighbor!"

The shepherd's eyes widened, and he asked, "*The* neighbor?"

The man smiled and nodded. Shamar was now excited too! He jumped up to greet the shepherd. "You must be the one who made the changes in Natan! You see, we have not been friends since I moved next to him years earlier. He told me that, after talking to you one evening, he wanted to apologize to me, and I forgave him. Whatever you said changed him, and now we have a wonderful friendship. We also found his nephew is marrying my granddaughter today! We came to the wedding together!"

Natan pleaded with the shepherd, "Please stay! Join us!"

The shepherd replied, "I wish I could, but I have my flock with me and only have time to sell my wool this morning and then must travel on. I'm sorry."

Shamar's eyes lit up! "My wife is in need of good wool to weave and spin before winter. May I see it?"

7th Commandment

Keep Promises To
Others And GOD

The three of them went to see the bundles of wool the shepherd had on his cart. They loved the feel and shine it had, and Shamar offered the shepherd a fair deal for all of it.

Meanwhile, Agape and Samantha were watching the wedding couple.

"She is beautiful," Sammy said. "They look so happy! What *is* a wedding, Agape?"

He knew about weddings from his shepherd and explained them to Sammy.

"When a man and a woman fall in love, they have a ceremony like this one. It is an oath before God that binds them together."

"Very good, Agape!" the shepherd said when he overheard what Agape had explained to Samantha. "This is also God's seventh commandment. When humans take this pledge to one another, they stay married for life, or they are breaking a promise with God."

Samantha thought to herself, *Oh, I like weddings! I wonder if sheep can be married too.*

The shepherd quickly went on to say, "The animal kingdom does not have weddings. Sheep, for example, pick out a mate they love and then stay together for life."

The shepherd continued, "That can be a long time, so it is good to pick out someone you think of as your best friend." He smiled at Sammy and Agape since they had the same thought going on in their minds.

The shepherd picked up the empty cart, and they all walked on that afternoon toward Neva. He felt peaceful thinking of how Shamar and Natan were now good friends, and it warmed his heart.

Agape and Samantha were silent, but both were thinking about what the shepherd explained about loving their best friend for a lifetime. Their hearts were warmed too!

Meeting Old Friends, Making New Ones

That afternoon, they arrived at Neva. The shepherd was going to buy supplies, and if they made good time, they would be home by nightfall. He bought several new tools and warm garments for winter days ahead and placed them in the cart. He went back to get a blanket and a bag of wheat.

As he was getting his coins out to pay, his flock started bleating loudly. He quickly turned around to make sure there was nothing there to harm them but saw only crowds of people walking by. He picked up his goods, and when he returned to the cart, he saw it was empty. The tools and garments were gone. Puzzled, he put his goods in the cart and looked around, wondering what had happened.

Someone grabbed his arm, and when he turned, he saw Vetri, her father, and her mother.

Her father seemed frantic as he told him, "Sir, we have just witnessed a man taking things from your cart! I did not know it was not his until you returned. We saw by your expression it belonged to you. I will gladly go with you and point him out!"

Vetri wanted to go along, but first, she asked, "Mother, please, may I go with them? I want to help."

Her father, very happy with the recent changes in his daughter, grabbed her in his arms, saying to the shepherd, "My wife will watch your cart, but let's go before I lose sight of him!"

The three left, hurrying down the crowded village as Vetri and her father watched for the man suspected of stealing.

Vetri's father spotted him and called out loudly to him, "Stop! We know that you are a thief!"

The man did not run away but turned, facing them. He said calmly, "Are you speaking to me, sir? I am no thief. I have not even been to the place of trading or selling today. I have only arrived here minutes ago. What are you saying?"

"No!" Vetri's father said confidently. "The three of us watched you with our own eyes remove the things from this man's cart!"

8th Commandment

Do Not Steal From Others

55

9th Commandment
Always Tell The Truth

56

The man laughed and said, "If that were so, where are these things you say I took?"

Vetri leaned over to the shepherd and whispered, "Sir, I saw this man too. He is the one who took your things from the cart!"

The shepherd smiled at Vetri for helping her father.

He walked over the man, looked him in the eyes, and said to him, "Sir, I will ask you if you stole my goods. Before you answer, I will tell you that there were three people who saw you do this. Stealing from someone is wrong. It is not only against man's law, but it is God's eighth commandment. It would be bad to sin, but if you were to lie about it, you would be breaking God's ninth commandment. I will ask you only for the truth, but remember, you are saying this to God and a young girl who is listening to your answer."

The man had never been confronted like that before. He could not speak as he looked in the eyes of the young child who innocently waited for the answer. Instead of speaking, he untied his long robe and removed the tools wrapped in the garments that he had tied with his sash. He handed all the stolen items to the shepherd, who could tell the man was ashamed.

The man looked down and then asked, "What are you going to do to me for stealing your goods?"

"Nothing, sir," the shepherd replied. "I have my goods returned to me, and I am sure God is smiling at you for doing the right thing."

Vetri smiled and chimed in, saying, "Me too!"

The man was grateful to all of them, and he was so overcome with the grace the shepherd gave to him that he apologized as tears rolled down his face.

The flock started bleating when they saw their shepherd returning, and he said to them, "I should have listened when you all warned me!" He laughed. He waved goodbye to Vetri, who was holding hands with her mother and her father and standing right by the grateful man.

They all waved to him and shouted, "Come back anytime, sir!"

"We will," the shepherd replied, "and, Vetri, thank you for being so helpful!"

On their way to Kerr, the shepherd explained the eighth and ninth commandments and how the man returned the shepherd's goods. He changed his heart when he confessed what he had done, not wanting to sin against God.

God had touched Vetri's heart, and she had changed also! The shepherd was amazed how she now respected her mother and her father just as they had *hoped* she would.

Good News in the Village of Kerr

The flock was excited to get back home, and they had made good time. If they walked fast, they could be there by nightfall. Sammy liked the idea of hurrying through Kerr. She was afraid of that large man behind the table.

When they went through Kerr, the large man and his table were no longer there. Many people were gathered around, listening to someone talking at the center of the village. The people were cheering for what was being said, so the shepherd stopped briefly to hear. To his surprise, the cheering was for the large man. He was being honored for something by three other men.

"We cannot tell you, Tarron, what this will mean for our village," one of the men said with gratitude.

A lady nearby saw the shepherd had just arrived and wanted to share what was going on. "Isn't it wonderful? Tarron has been a businessman here many years, and not one person got along well with him. The shepherds and the farmers never got a fair price for their goods. His temper made him rude to people, and the children were always scared of him."

The shepherd looked at Sammy and added, "So are my sheep!"

She laughed and continued, "He has been going around apologizing to everyone for a long while now for his cursing and cheating people to make more money. No one believed him at first because he has always wanted to be the richest man. Today he closed his trade, and he gave almost all of his riches to the village for a church!"

The shepherd was touched by the change in the man. He smiled and said to the woman, "God bless him for his bighearted *charity*."

The shepherd called to his sheep, and they followed him out.

Tarron noticed the shepherd as he passed by. He waved and smiled at him, yelling, "Sir! You were right. We can always change!"

The shepherd nodded to him and smiled back, saying, "So I see! God works all things for the good!"

Sammy even walked closer to him on her way out, sensing the goodness that was in him now.

Home, Sweet Home

The sheep and lambs were playing and grazing and enjoying being home, and there was a nice rainfall that morning. Agape still liked splashing in puddles as he walked with his shepherd, who was counting his flock.

Agape came across the biggest puddle he had ever seen. He was just ready to jump in when he saw his reflection for the first time. "Is that really me?" he questioned as he studied himself. His wool had grown out, but it was still very uneven in many places, and his shaved spot was not growing in well. *I should remember to hold still at the next shearing*, he thought. Then he noticed that, although his horns had grown and were starting to curl up a little, they were not at all what he thought they would look like. They were certainly not as splendid as those of some of the other rams in the flock. Their horns were much larger and absolutely majestic to see! Then he saw it—his black ear! *No wonder Sammy teases me!* he thought. *It's not only black, but it droops down too.*

A tear rolled down Agape's face and landed in the puddle, making it ripple. When the ripples cleared, Agape was still staring into the puddle, along with his shepherd, who knelt beside him.

The shepherd knew what Agape was thinking about and tenderly asked him anyway, "Agape, what are you thinking about that makes you so sad?"

Agape just stared at his reflection and wondered why the shepherd would ever think he was *unique*. Couldn't he see?

"Agape," the shepherd said again, "I think you are thinking things you shouldn't be thinking."

Just look at me, Agape thought with a pout. *I'm a real mess! My horns are not as big as the other rams'. My fleece is uneven, and I have this droopy black ear! I wish I were like the others.*

The shepherd shook his head and said, "When you want anything others have that you don't have, you are *coveting* the things you wish for. That is breaking the tenth commandment. God wants us to be happy with what he gave us and not wish to have what he gave others. I love my entire flock. Everyone is different, but I look at them

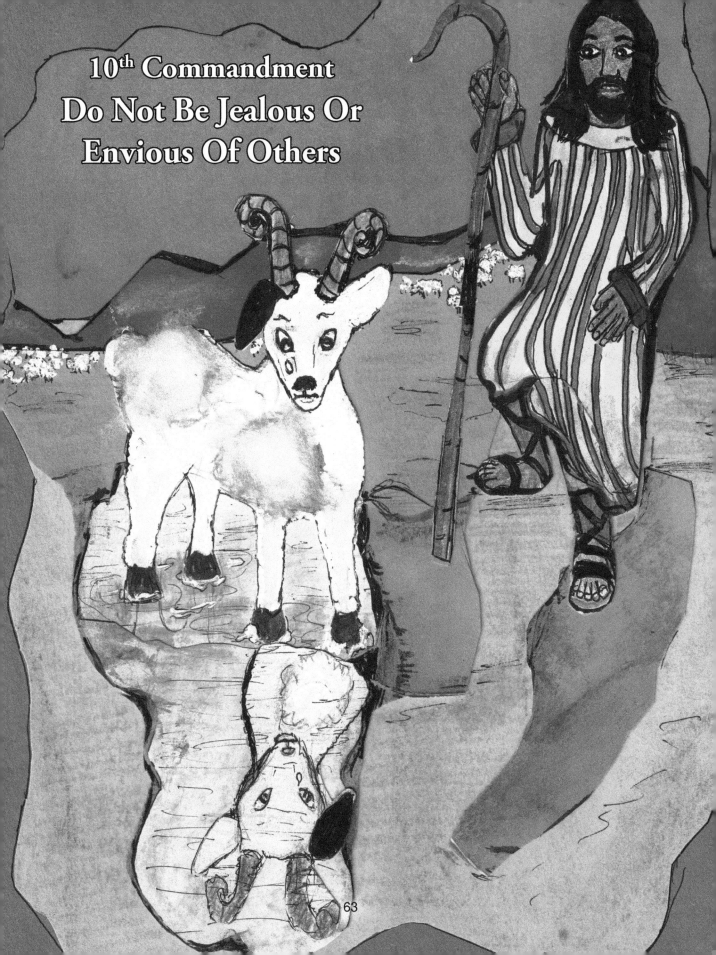

10th Commandment
Do Not Be Jealous Or
Envious Of Others

63

like God looks at his children. *He* doesn't look at the outside. *He* looks at the inside. *He* looks at their heart. When I see you, I see the best kind of heart. It's big, pure, and full of love for everyone. That's why the whole flock likes you, Agape. They are looking at your inside. You are *unique* just the way you are!"

Agape felt elated at the kind words from his shepherd and knew it was the truth coming from him. Agape's heart was racing as he thought, *I know exactly what he means! I love my shepherd, and I love Sammy for who they are on the inside, not the outside!*

The shepherd saw Sammy coming their way. He smiled. "Agape, Sammy is coming. Why don't you tell *her* how you *love* her?"

He wagged his bobbed tail and bounced down the hill to meet his best friend.

The shepherd stood up and watched them. He could not help smiling. Sammy bleated out to Agape the sweetest joyful sound. The shepherd knew she was saying "I love you too!" Soon all the sheep were joining in their happy bleating!

The shepherd returned to the sheepfold entrance to get some rest. His prayers of thanks were overflowing to God, who gave him so many blessings every day. Tonight, he said a special prayer for Agape and Samantha, who were going to be together for life. He knew he would miss Agape, his *unique* little shadow, but was filled with joy at his happiness.

The next morning, the shepherd awoke, stretched, rubbed his eyes, and reached for his sturdy staff when he felt something familiar and smiled the biggest smile. There right by his side was his little shadow—sound asleep. Right beside him was Sammy, who would be his second shadow.

The shepherd said another quick prayer to God, "Thank *you, my Father*!" He lay back down and scratched Agape's ear as they all slept in.

THE GREATEST COMMANDMENT

Love the LORD your GOD with all your heart, with all your soul and with all your mind

Agape's Surprise

That autumn things sure had changed! Sammy was going to have a lamb any day, and Agape was delighted about becoming a father. The shepherd, as well as Ana-is, noticed that Sammy was a lot bigger than any other ewes that were lambing.

It was a cool, starry evening with her shepherd there to help and protect her when Sammy had her lamb. She didn't have one, she didn't have two, but she had three lambs! The shepherd praised God that Sammy and the triplets were all healthy, and then he called for Agape.

Agape was anxious to see Sammy and their lamb but was surprised when he saw three!

"Well, black ear," Sammy proudly asked, "what do you think?"

Agape looked at all three lambs in confusion. "Which one is ours?" he thought.

"Meet your daughters!" Sammy laughed.

Agape was so overwhelmed with joy he could only think, "Sammy! They're beautiful! They all look just like you!"

The shepherd was laughing, too, and said, "Agape, look closer. They look a lot like you too!"

Agape walked in closer and was beaming. One daughter's left ear was black. Another daughter had two black ears! The third little girl's right ear was black, just like his! Agape's heart was melting with love for his new family.

The shepherd teased Sammy, this time asking her, "We certainly can't call everyone around here black ear! Do you have names for the little ones?"

Sammy already loved names that her shepherd taught them while traveling through the villages, and he already knew what Sammy was thinking.

He said to her, "We all believe, so we all have *faith*. We can name this sweet lamb Faith," picking up the lamb with a left black ear. "This little beauty with two black ears is Hope since we all need *hope*. Agape's 'shadow,'" he continued, picking up the lamb with the black right ear, "will be named Charity. The name Charity actually means 'love,' just like your name, Agape!"

They were all overcome with joy as they thanked God for their newest blessings.

"And now abideth faith, hope, and charity, these
three; but the greatest of these is charity."
—1 Corinthians 13:13 (KJV)

About the Author

Di Abele is a recently retired dental assistant. She and her husband, Walt, live in the equestrian community of Pine Ridge, in Beverly Hills, Florida, with their Great Pyrenees, Snowy. Di has one daughter, Shannon, who is married to Zach, and they have three children: James, Molly, and Abby.

During the COVID-19 lockdown, Di was inspired to write and illustrate her first Christian book for children. Her main goal for the story was to deliver an allegory of Jesus and his children using Agape and his shepherd to better understand the nature of Jesus.

Di is a member of Gulf to Lake Church in Crystal River, Florida. She is also a member of Hands of Praise, a growing worship arts ministry that includes interpretative sign language, dance, and more. She enjoys animals, sketching, painting, gardening, walking, and reading.

CPSIA information can be obtained
at www.ICGtesting.com
Printed in the USA
LVHW070712110522
718475LV00007B/179